OCT 2005

WELCOME TO THE U.S.A.
NEBRASKA

Written by Ann Heinrichs   Illustrated by Matt Kania
Content Adviser: Sally Snyder, Coordinator of Children and Young
Adult Services, Nebraska Library Commission, Lincoln, Nebraska

Published in the United States of America by The Child's World®
PO Box 326 • Chanhassen, MN 55317-0326
800-599-READ • www.childsworld.com

Photo Credits
Cover: Digital Visions; frontispiece: Photodisc.

Interior: Affinity Snacks: 33; Agate Fossil Beds National Monument: 6; Corbis: 10 (James L. Amos), 13 (Jim Richardson), 18 (Tom Bean); M. Forsberg/Nebraska DED/Nebraska Division of Tourism and Travel: 26, 34; Philip Gould/Corbis: 21, 30; Nebraska Division of Tourism and Travel: 9 (J. Nabb), 25 (G. Ryan/Nebraska DED); NEBRASKAland Magazine/Nebraska Game and Parks Commission: 14; Offutt Air Force Base: 29; Erik Stenbakken/stenbakken.com/Nebraska Division of Tourism and Travel: 17, 22.

Acknowledgments
The Child's World®: Mary Berendes, Publishing Director

Editorial Directions, Inc.: E. Russell Primm, Editorial Director; Katie Marsico, Associate Editor; Judith Shiffer, Assistant Editor; Matt Messbarger, Editorial Assistant; Susan Hindman, Copy Editor; Melissa McDaniel, Proofreader; Kevin Cunningham, Peter Garnham, Matt Messbarger, Olivia Nellums, Chris Simms, Molly Symmonds, Katherine Trickle, Carl Stephen Wender, Fact Checkers; Tim Griffin/IndexServ, Indexer; Cian Loughlin O'Day, Photo Researcher and Editor

The Design Lab: Kathleen Petelinsek, Design; Julia Goozen, Art Production

Library of Congress Cataloging-in-Publication Data
Heinrichs, Ann.
  Nebraska / by Ann Heinrichs.
    p. cm. — (Welcome to the U.S.A.)
  Includes index.
  ISBN 1-59296-448-6 (library bound : alk. paper) 1. Nebraska—Juvenile literature.
I. Title.
  F666.3.H453 2006
  978.2—dc22   2005000528

Ann Heinrichs is the author of more than 100 books for children and young adults. She has also enjoyed successful careers as a children's book editor and an advertising copywriter. Ann grew up in Fort Smith, Arkansas, and lives in Chicago, Illinois.

About the Author
Ann Heinrichs

Matt Kania loves maps and, as a kid, dreamed of making them. In school he studied geography and cartography, and today he makes maps for a living. Matt's favorite thing about drawing maps is learning about the places they represent. Many of the maps he has created can be found in books, magazines, videos, Web sites, and public places.

About the
Map Illustrator
Matt Kania

On the cover: **Chimney Rock draws visitors to Nebraska.**
On page one: **Omaha has beautiful parks and tall buildings.**

OUR NEBRASKA TRIP

Nebraska's Nickname:
The Cornhusker State

R eady for a trip through Nebraska? You're in for quite a ride! You'll hang out with fur traders and cowboys. You'll watch dancing birds and trick dogs. You'll feed fish and cluck like a chicken. You'll see golden wheat fields and grazing cattle. And you'll see skeletons millions of years old. Not bad for one state!

Just follow that dotted line or skip around. Either way, you're in for an exciting tour. Are you all buckled up? Then we're on our way!

WELCOME TO NEBRASKA

As you travel through Nebraska, watch for all the interesting facts along the way.

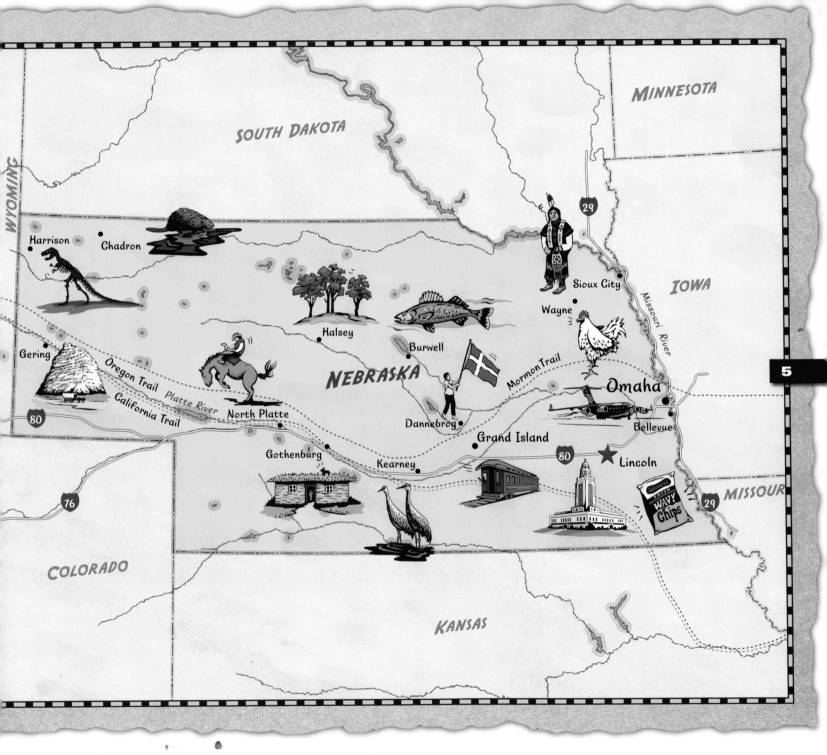

MINNESOTA

SOUTH DAKOTA

WYOMING

Harrison

Chadron

IOWA

29

Sioux City

Wayne

Missouri River

Gering

Halsey

Burwell

NEBRASKA

Mormon Trail

Omaha

Oregon Trail Platte River

North Platte

Dannebrog

Bellevue

California Trail

80

Grand Island

Gothenburg

Kearney

80

Lincoln

MISSOURI

76

Nahrwald's FRESH WAVY Chips

29

COLORADO

KANSAS

Oink, oink! Check out the *Dinohyus* skeleton at Agate Fossil Beds!

Scientists found hundreds of skeletons at Agate Fossil Beds. They include huge beavers and tiny deer.

6

Scary skeletons are everywhere! Watch out for that *Dinohyus*. Its name means "terrible hog." And steer clear of that *Moropus*. This enormous horse stands on its hind legs.

You're at Agate **Fossil** Beds. It's in far-western Nebraska, near Harrison. The scary skeletons are in the visitors' center. Scientists dug them up from the surrounding area.

The animals are about 20 million years old. What happened to them? Scientists believe Nebraska was having a **drought.** Thirsty animals gathered at a water hole here. Slowly it dried up, and they died.

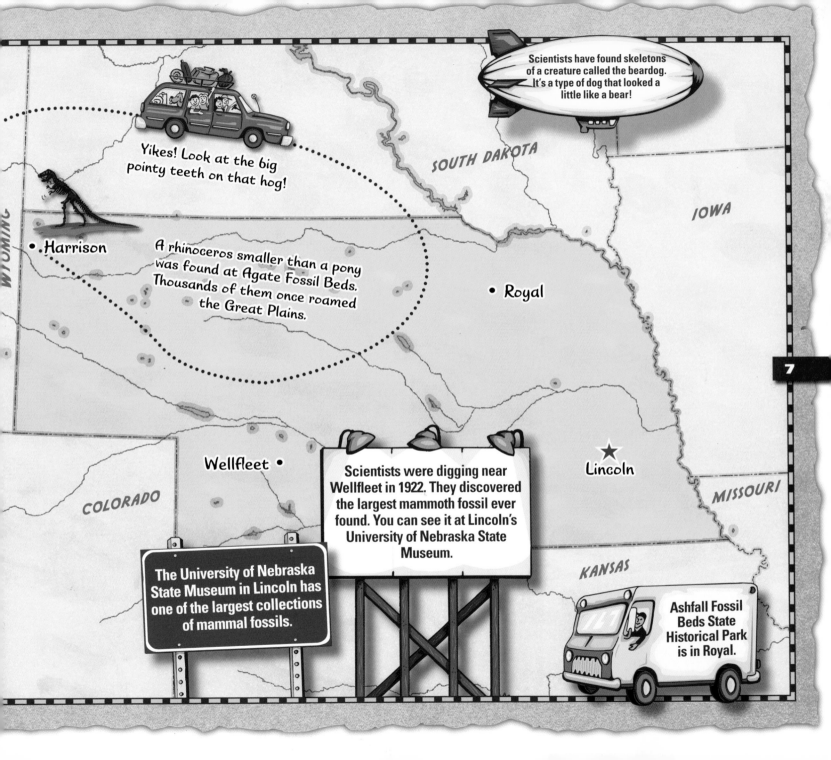

Scientists have found skeletons of a creature called the beardog. It's a type of dog that looked a little like a bear!

SOUTH DAKOTA

IOWA

Yikes! Look at the big pointy teeth on that hog!

WYOMING

• Harrison

A rhinoceros smaller than a pony was found at Agate Fossil Beds. Thousands of them once roamed the Great Plains.

• Royal

7

Wellfleet •

★ Lincoln

COLORADO

Scientists were digging near Wellfleet in 1922. They discovered the largest mammoth fossil ever found. You can see it at Lincoln's University of Nebraska State Museum.

MISSOURI

KANSAS

The University of Nebraska State Museum in Lincoln has one of the largest collections of mammal fossils.

Ashfall Fossil Beds State Historical Park is in Royal.

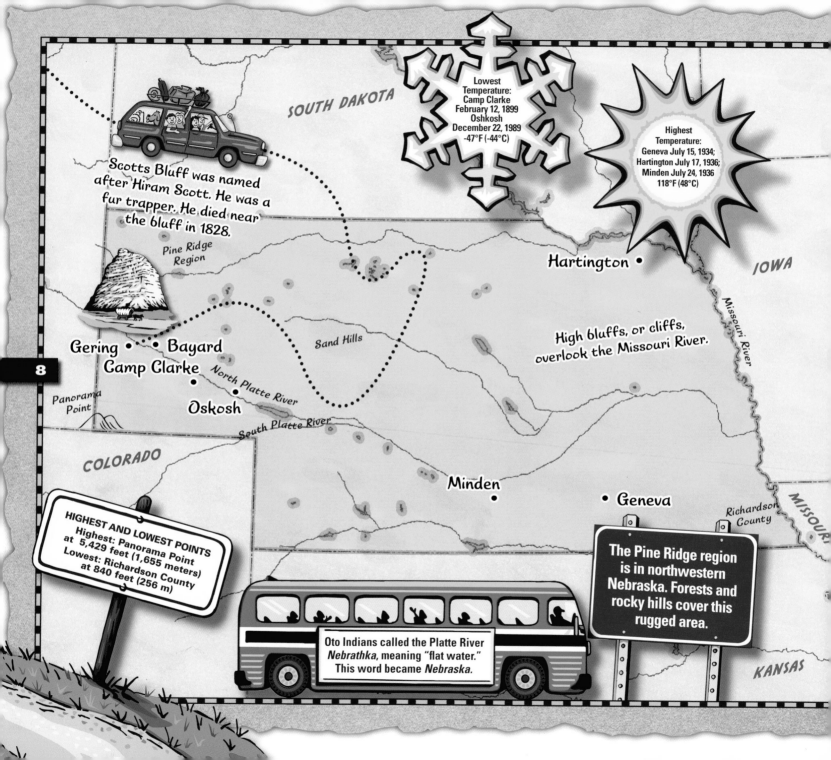

SOUTH DAKOTA

IOWA

Lowest Temperature:
Camp Clarke
February 12, 1899
Oshkosh
December 22, 1989
-47°F (-44°C)

Highest Temperature:
Geneva July 15, 1934;
Hartington July 17, 1936;
Minden July 24, 1936
118°F (48°C)

Scotts Bluff was named after Hiram Scott. He was a fur trapper. He died near the bluff in 1828.

Pine Ridge Region

Hartington

High bluffs, or cliffs, overlook the Missouri River.

Missouri River

Gering • Bayard
Camp Clarke

Sand Hills

Panorama Point

North Platte River

Oskosh

South Platte River

COLORADO

Minden

Geneva

Richardson County

MISSOURI

HIGHEST AND LOWEST POINTS
Highest: Panorama Point
at 5,429 feet (1,655 meters)
Lowest: Richardson County
at 840 feet (256 m)

The Pine Ridge region is in northwestern Nebraska. Forests and rocky hills cover this rugged area.

Oto Indians called the Platte River Nebrathka, meaning "flat water." This word became Nebraska.

KANSAS

Scotts Bluff near Gering

Imagine you're a **pioneer** headed west. You would know you'd arrived at Scotts Bluff. These rocky cliffs rise high over the plains. You might have seen Chimney Rock, near Bayard. These tall rock formations rise in western Nebraska.

Rolling plains cover most of Nebraska. They make rich farmland and grazing land. The Sand Hills are in north-central Nebraska. Here, wind has blown the sandy soil into piles.

The Platte River is Nebraska's major river. It begins where two rivers join. They are the North Platte and the South Platte. The Platte River flows into the Missouri River. The Missouri forms Nebraska's eastern border.

A covered wagon travels past Chimney Rock. Would you have made a good pioneer?

Mitchell Pass is an opening through Scotts Bluff. Pioneers began traveling through the pass in 1852.

These sandhill cranes call the Platte River home.

About half a million sandhill cranes stay along the Platte River from February through April.

Dancing Cranes by the Platte River

The long-legged birds stretch out their wings. They gracefully bow down to each other. Then they spring high into the air!

You're watching the dance of the sandhill cranes. These awesome birds gather along the Platte River. Many of them can be seen east of Kearney. They feed in the cornfields. They dance to attract a mate.

Many other animals live in Nebraska all year. They include deer, prairie dogs, badgers, and coyotes.

Nebraska doesn't have much forestland. Prairies once covered much of the state. Prairies are grasslands where tall grasses grow. But farmers plowed up much of these grasslands.

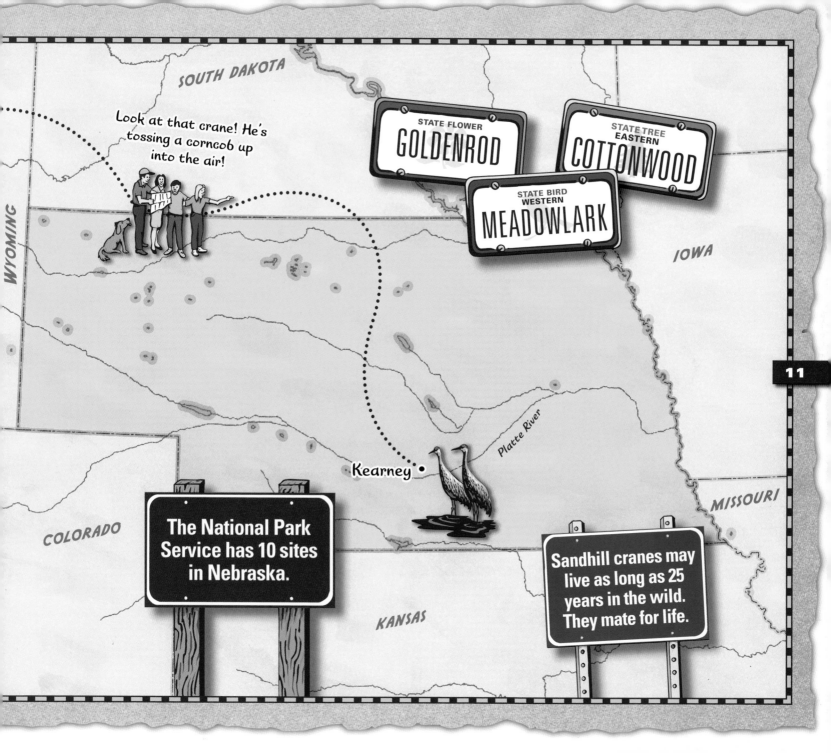

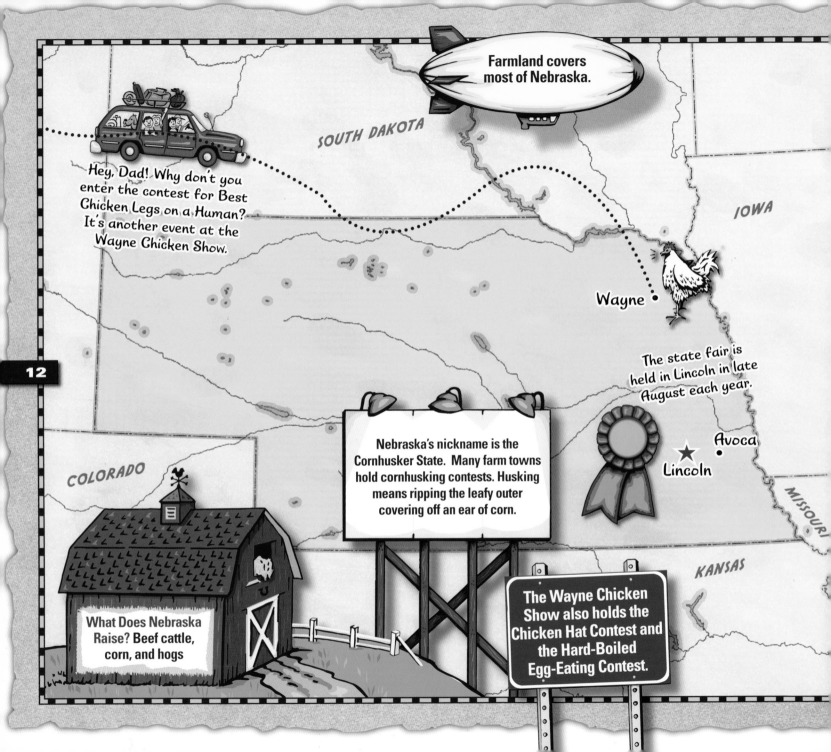

Farmland covers most of Nebraska.

SOUTH DAKOTA

IOWA

Hey, Dad! Why don't you enter the contest for Best Chicken Legs on a Human? It's another event at the Wayne Chicken Show.

Wayne

The state fair is held in Lincoln in late August each year.

Avoca

Lincoln

COLORADO

Nebraska's nickname is the Cornhusker State. Many farm towns hold cornhusking contests. Husking means ripping the leafy outer covering off an ear of corn.

MISSOURI

KANSAS

What Does Nebraska Raise? Beef cattle, corn, and hogs

The Wayne Chicken Show also holds the Chicken Hat Contest and the Hard-Boiled Egg-Eating Contest.

The Wayne Chicken Show

Would you like to enter the National Cluck-Off? You don't have to do much. Just act and sound like a chicken. And keep it up for fifteen seconds!

It all happens at the Wayne Chicken Show. This festival celebrates a favorite Nebraska farm animal.

Nebraska is one of the top farming states. Fields of wheat stretch across the western plains. The north-central region is good for grazing cattle. Farmers in the east grow many different crops.

Beef cattle are Nebraska's most valuable farm animals. Hogs are important, too. Farmers sell their meat all over the country. Corn is the state's leading crop. Farmers also raise wheat, soybeans, and hay.

A Nebraska farmer harvests his corn crop.

Avoca holds the Quack-Off Duck Race every year.

Scientists from Calamus Fish Hatchery release walleye into a reservoir.

Calamus Fish Hatchery has 24 raceways and 51 ponds.

Calamus Fish Hatchery in Burwell

Where do fish come from? From rivers, lakes, and oceans, of course! But those aren't the only fish homes. Some fish come from hatcheries. Hatcheries are like big fish farms!

Just visit Calamus State Fish Hatchery in Burwell. It grows trout, bass, perch, and other fish. Workers watch over thousands of fish eggs. Small fish, called fry, hatch from the eggs. When they're a little bigger, they're called fingerlings.

The fish swim in long tanks called raceways. In one raceway, you can feed the fish. You may be eating those fish one day! The hatchery releases full-grown fish into lakes and streams.

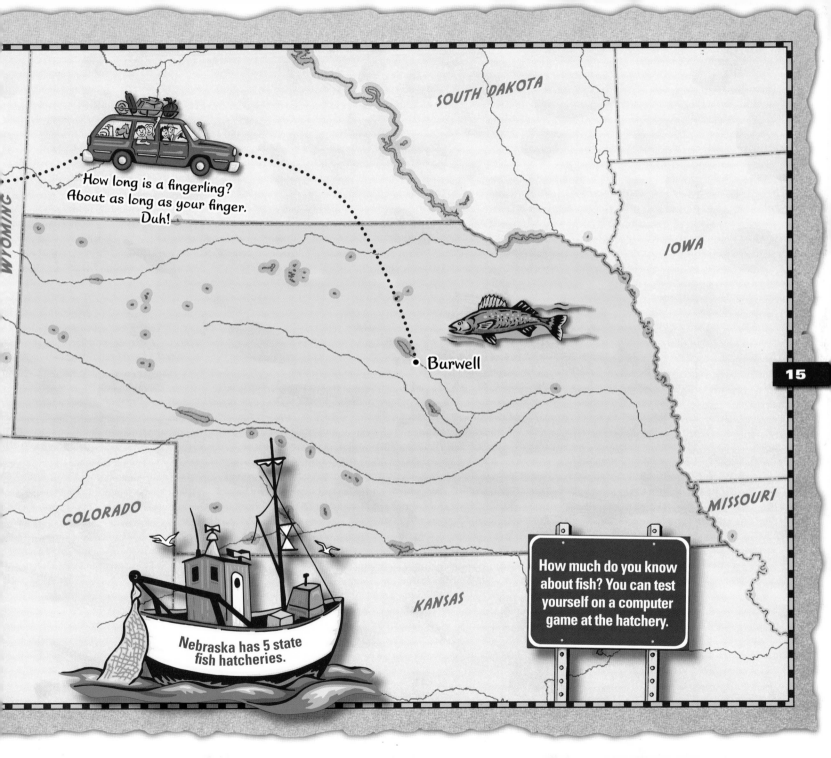

How long is a fingerling? About as long as your finger. Duh!

SOUTH DAKOTA

WYOMING

IOWA

• Burwell

COLORADO

MISSOURI

KANSAS

Nebraska has 5 state fish hatcheries.

How much do you know about fish? You can test yourself on a computer game at the hatchery.

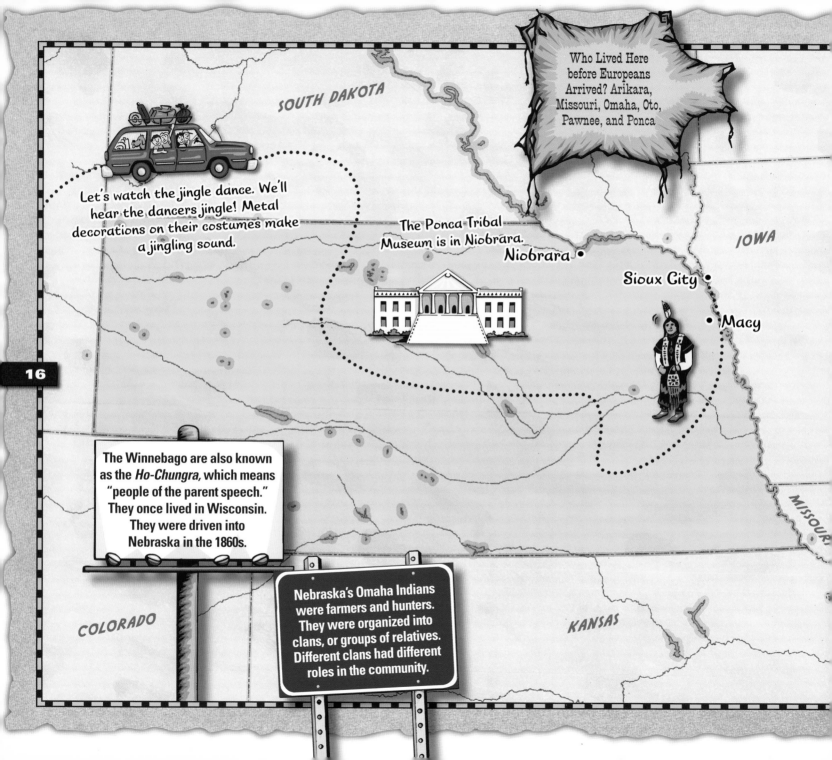

SOUTH DAKOTA

IOWA

MISSOURI

COLORADO

KANSAS

Who Lived Here before Europeans Arrived? Arikara, Missouri, Omaha, Oto, Pawnee, and Ponca

Let's watch the jingle dance. We'll hear the dancers jingle! Metal decorations on their costumes make a jingling sound.

The Ponca Tribal Museum is in Niobrara.

Niobrara •

Sioux City •

• Macy

The Winnebago are also known as the *Ho-Chungra,* which means "people of the parent speech." They once lived in Wisconsin. They were driven into Nebraska in the 1860s.

Nebraska's Omaha Indians were farmers and hunters. They were organized into clans, or groups of relatives. Different clans had different roles in the community.

The Winnebago Powwow

The dancers wear colorful feathers and beads. Fringe and feathers swirl around as they dance. This is the Winnebago Powwow. Winnebago Indians hold this festival every year near Sioux City. They perform many **traditional** dances.

Many American Indian groups once lived in Nebraska. Some hunted buffalo across the plains. They lived in teepees made of animal skins. Others lived in earth lodges. They hunted and grew corn and other vegetables.

French explorers crossed Nebraska in 1739. Soon French fur trappers and traders arrived. They traded with the Indians for furs. Nebraska became part of the United States in 1803.

This Omaha Indian is attending a powwow in Macy.

Ready to trade some furs? This reconstructed trading post in located in Chadron.

The Oregon Trail ran from Independence, Missouri, to Oregon, on the west coast.

Fur Trade Days in Chadron

Put on your **buckskins.** It's time for Fur Trade Days! Chadron holds this festival every year. People dress like 1800s fur traders. They put up tents just like fur traders did. They enjoy shooting demonstrations, music, parades, and fireworks.

Trappers and traders were Nebraska's early explorers. They made trails along the Platte River. Chimney Rock and Scotts Bluff were important landmarks. Later, pioneers would follow the traders' pathways. One major route became the Oregon Trail.

Fur companies began setting up trading posts. Bellevue began as a fur-trading post in 1823. It was Nebraska's first permanent settlement.

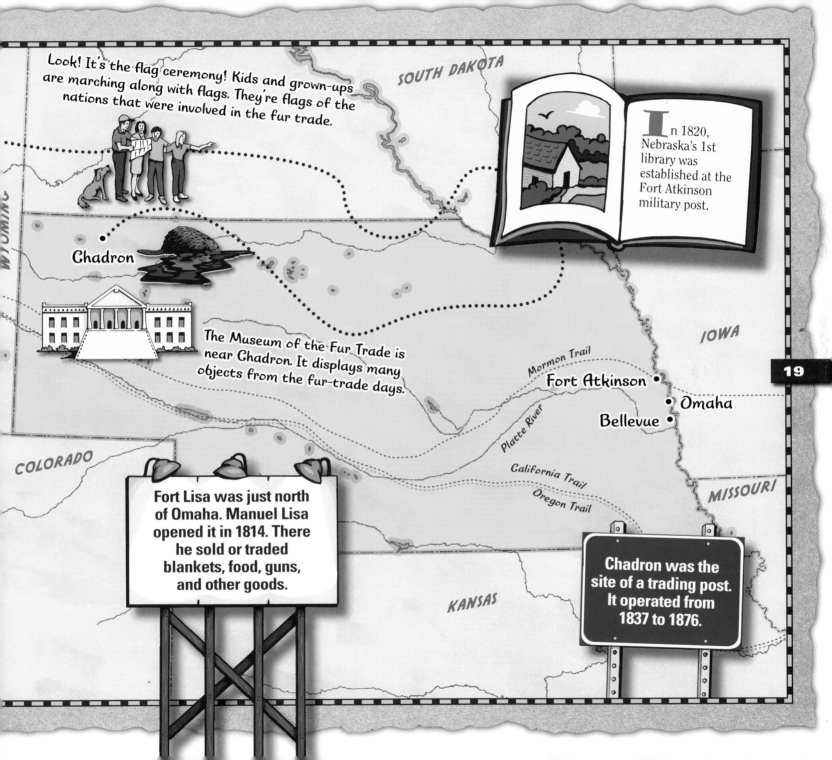

Look! It's the flag ceremony! Kids and grown-ups are marching along with flags. They're flags of the nations that were involved in the fur trade.

SOUTH DAKOTA

In 1820, Nebraska's 1st library was established at the Fort Atkinson military post.

WYOMING

Chadron

IOWA

The Museum of the Fur Trade is near Chadron. It displays many objects from the fur-trade days.

Mormon Trail

Fort Atkinson •

• Omaha

Bellevue •

Platte River

COLORADO

California Trail

Oregon Trail

MISSOURI

Fort Lisa was just north of Omaha. Manuel Lisa opened it in 1814. There he sold or traded blankets, food, guns, and other goods.

Chadron was the site of a trading post. It operated from 1837 to 1876.

KANSAS

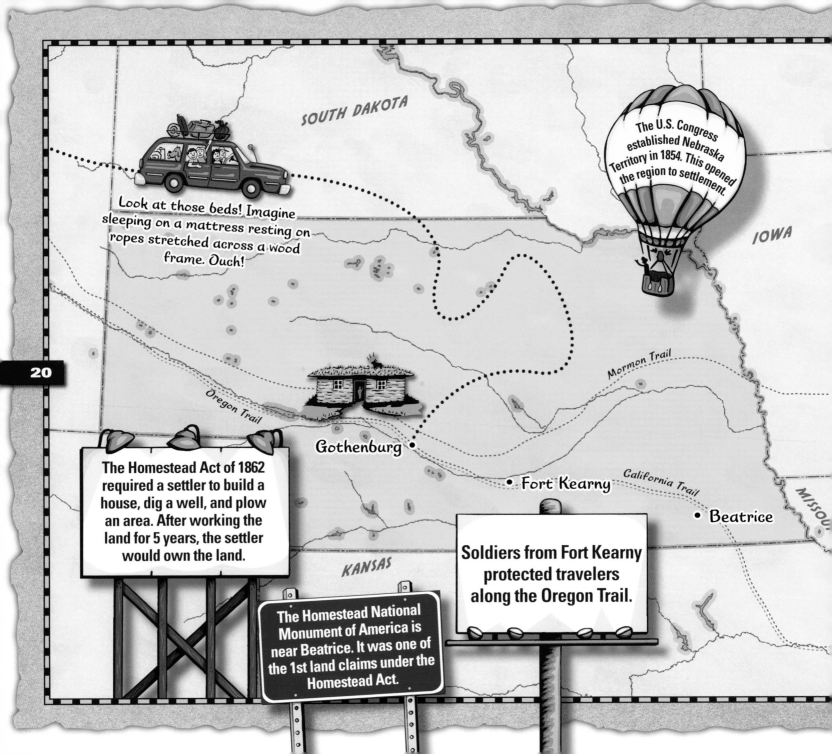

SOUTH DAKOTA

IOWA

Look at those beds! Imagine sleeping on a mattress resting on ropes stretched across a wood frame. Ouch!

The U.S. Congress established Nebraska Territory in 1854. This opened the region to settlement.

Mormon Trail

Oregon Trail

Gothenburg

Fort Kearny

California Trail

Beatrice

MISSOURI

The Homestead Act of 1862 required a settler to build a house, dig a well, and plow an area. After working the land for 5 years, the settler would own the land.

KANSAS

The Homestead National Monument of America is near Beatrice. It was one of the 1st land claims under the Homestead Act.

Soldiers from Fort Kearny protected travelers along the Oregon Trail.

Gothenburg's Sod House Museum

Plants are growing on the roof. The walls are built of **sod.** Inside, the floors are powdery dirt. This is a sod house. It's part of Gothenburg's Sod House Museum.

Early settlers in Nebraska built sod homes. They found few trees for building houses. Many settlers had come over the Oregon Trail. They hauled all they owned in covered wagons. The wagon wheels left deep ruts, or grooves. You can still see those wheel ruts today.

In 1862, the U.S. government passed the Homestead Act. It offered free land to settlers. Then thousands of pioneers poured into Nebraska.

There's no place like home! Visit the Sod House Museum to learn how early settlers lived.

Pioneers took the Oregon, California, and Mormon trails through Nebraska.

Grundlovs Fest in Dannebrog

Want to dance? Just stop by Wilbur's Czech festival!

Grundlovs Fest is also called Danish Day. It honors the signing of Denmark's constitution, or basic set of laws, in 1849.

Take a pony ride. Gobble up some Danish pastries. Then watch the costumed dancers whirl around. You're enjoying Grundlovs Fest in Dannebrog!

This festival celebrates the town's Danish **heritage.** (The word *Danish* means things related to Denmark.)

Immigrants from many lands settled in Nebraska. Many towns still celebrate their settlers' heritage. For example, Wilber holds a Czech festival. Grand Island holds a German Heritage Day. One event is the Running of the Wieners. It's a race for dachshunds. They're often called wiener dogs. Why? Because their bodies are long—like wieners!

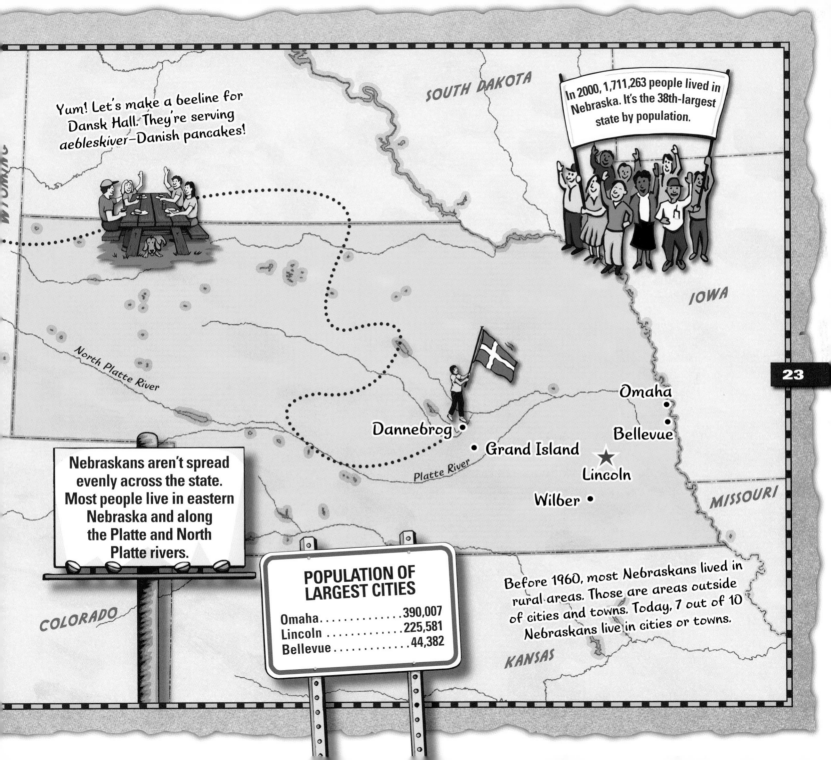

Yum! Let's make a beeline for Dansk Hall. They're serving aebleskiver–Danish pancakes!

In 2000, 1,711,263 people lived in Nebraska. It's the 38th-largest state by population.

Nebraskans aren't spread evenly across the state. Most people live in eastern Nebraska and along the Platte and North Platte rivers.

POPULATION OF LARGEST CITIES

Omaha 390,007
Lincoln 225,581
Bellevue 44,382

Before 1960, most Nebraskans lived in rural areas. Those are areas outside of cities and towns. Today, 7 out of 10 Nebraskans live in cities or towns.

SOUTH DAKOTA

WYOMING

IOWA

North Platte River

Dannebrog

Grand Island

Platte River

Omaha

Bellevue

Lincoln

Wilber

MISSOURI

COLORADO

KANSAS

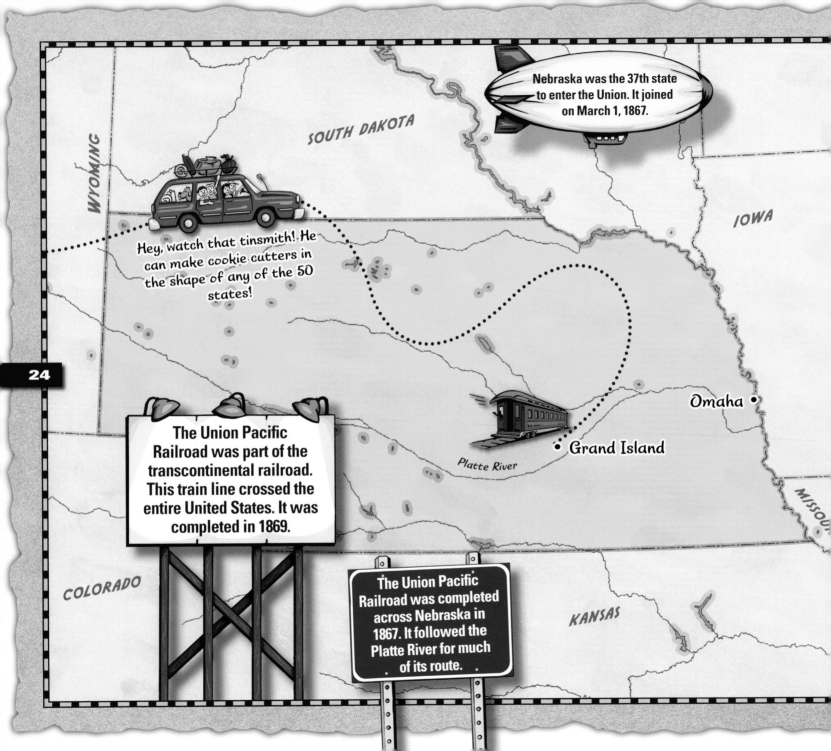

24

Meet the blacksmith and the tinsmith. Stop by the hatmaker's shop. Or just drop into someone's home. You're visiting Stuhr Museum of the Prairie Pioneer. It's built like a Nebraska prairie community. Many towns like this sprang up along train routes.

Railroads first crossed Nebraska in 1867. Then pioneers began arriving by train. Some opened shops in the new towns. Others plowed and planted crops.

Grasshoppers swarmed across the land in the 1870s. They destroyed acres of crops. Many farmers left the state.

Would you have liked living in a prairie community? Visit Grand Island and find out!

The Union Pacific Historical Collection includes uniforms, dining-car china, and model trains. It's on display in Omaha's Durham Western Heritage Museum.

A colorfully costumed Mexican dancer performs at Nebraskaland Days.

The Buffalo Bill Rodeo is named for William Cody. He was known as Buffalo Bill. His ranch is in North Platte.

Nebraskaland Days in North Platte

Cowboys cling for their life to bucking **broncos.** Other cowboys are riding bulls or roping calves. You're watching the Buffalo Bill Rodeo! It's part of North Platte's Nebraskaland Days celebration. Besides the rodeo, there are parades, shoot-outs, and barbecues.

You can have lots of fun in Nebraska. Most counties have fairs in the summer. Thousands of people attend Lincoln's Nebraska State Fair.

Campers and hikers enjoy the Pine Ridge Region. This forested area is in western Nebraska. Many people head for the Platte or Niobrara rivers. They go fishing or just enjoy nature.

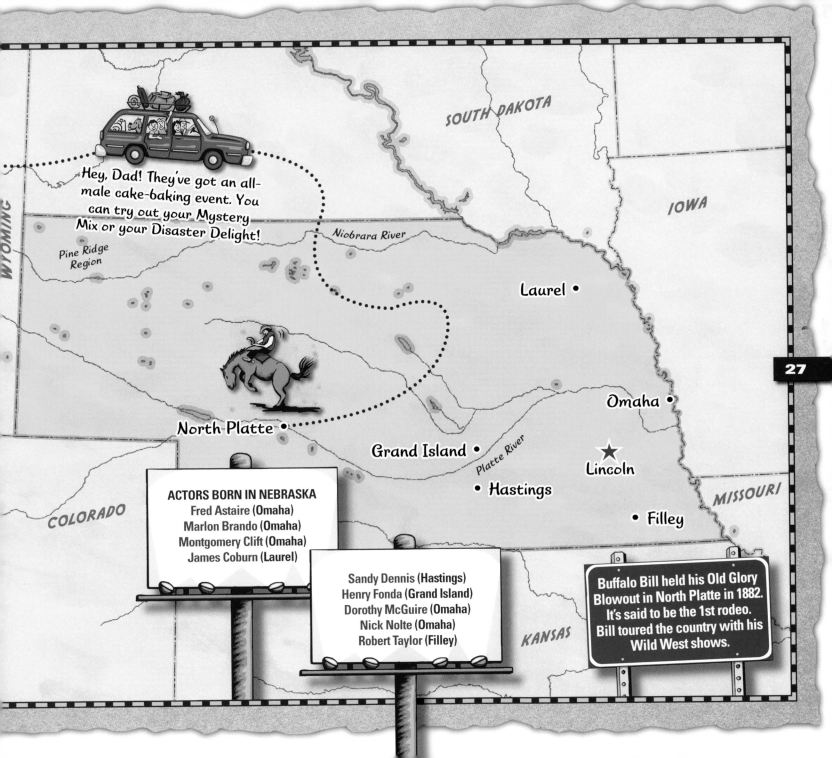

Hey, Dad! They've got an all-male cake-baking event. You can try out your Mystery Mix or your Disaster Delight!

SOUTH DAKOTA

IOWA

WYOMING

Pine Ridge Region

Niobrara River

Laurel •

Omaha •

North Platte •

Grand Island •

Platte River

★
Lincoln

MISSOURI

• Hastings

• Filley

COLORADO

ACTORS BORN IN NEBRASKA
Fred Astaire **(Omaha)**
Marlon Brando **(Omaha)**
Montgomery Clift **(Omaha)**
James Coburn **(Laurel)**

Sandy Dennis **(Hastings)**
Henry Fonda **(Grand Island)**
Dorothy McGuire **(Omaha)**
Nick Nolte **(Omaha)**
Robert Taylor **(Filley)**

KANSAS

Buffalo Bill held his Old Glory Blowout in North Platte in 1882. It's said to be the 1st rodeo. Bill toured the country with his Wild West shows.

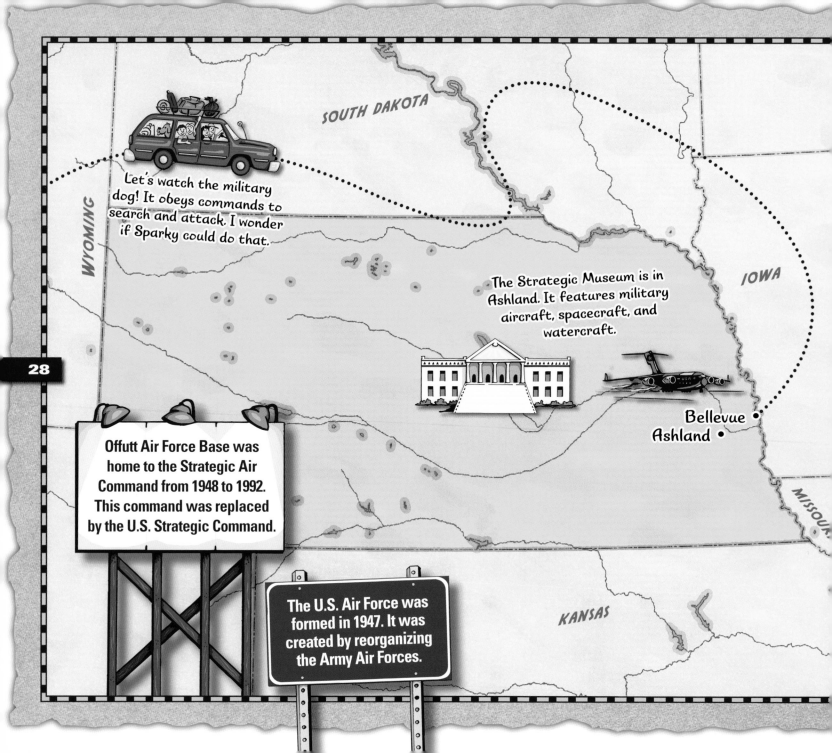

SOUTH DAKOTA

Let's watch the military dog! It obeys commands to search and attack. I wonder if Sparky could do that.

WYOMING

IOWA

The Strategic Museum is in Ashland. It features military aircraft, spacecraft, and watercraft.

Bellevue •
Ashland •

MISSOURI

Offutt Air Force Base was home to the Strategic Air Command from 1948 to 1992. This command was replaced by the U.S. Strategic Command.

The U.S. Air Force was formed in 1947. It was created by reorganizing the Army Air Forces.

KANSAS

Look out from the aircraft control tower. Chat with firefighters in the fire department. Visit the weather station. Then watch a military dog follow commands.

You're touring Offutt Air Force Base in Bellevue. It's home to the U.S. Strategic Command. This center controls the nation's **nuclear** forces.

Nebraska developed many new **industries** in the 1900s. Offutt Air Force Base employed hundreds of people. Many insurance companies made Nebraska their **headquarters,** too. Oil became an important industry in southeast Nebraska. And factories opened throughout the state.

Roger! This technician works at the Offutt aircraft control tower.

Lawmakers are busy inside Lincoln's skyscraper capitol.

Most state capitols are just a few stories high. But Nebraska's capitol is a **skyscraper.** Its office tower is fourteen stories high.

Inside are many state government offices. Nebraska has three branches of government. One branch makes the state's laws. It's called the state legislature. Nebraska's legislature is unusual, just like its capitol. All the other states have a two-house legislature. But not Nebraska. Its legislature has only one house.

The governor heads another branch of government. It carries out the laws. Courts make up the third branch. They decide whether someone has broken the law.

William Jennings Bryan ran for president 3 times and lost. His home is in Lincoln.

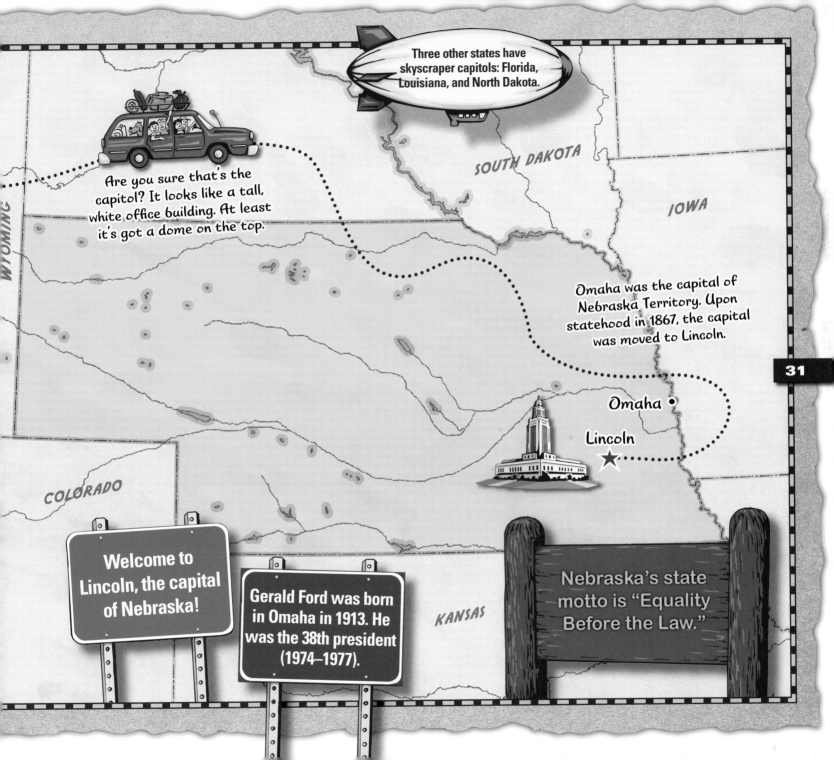

Three other states have skyscraper capitols: Florida, Louisiana, and North Dakota.

SOUTH DAKOTA

IOWA

WYOMING

Are you sure that's the capitol? It looks like a tall, white office building. At least it's got a dome on the top.

Omaha was the capital of Nebraska Territory. Upon statehood in 1867, the capital was moved to Lincoln.

Omaha •

Lincoln ★

COLORADO

Welcome to Lincoln, the capital of Nebraska!

Gerald Ford was born in Omaha in 1913. He was the 38th president (1974–1977).

KANSAS

Nebraska's state motto is "Equality Before the Law."

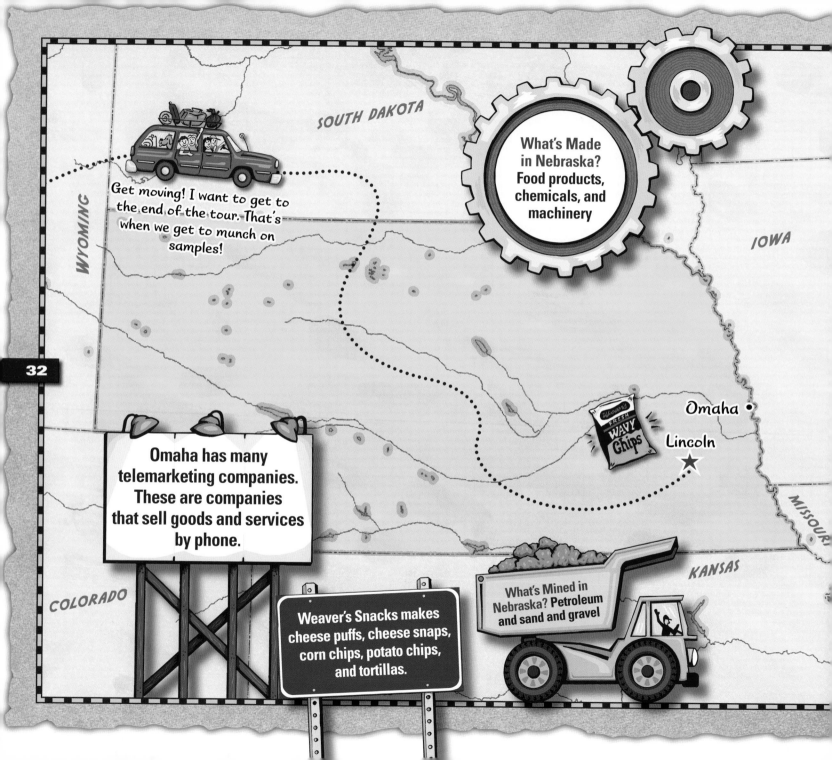

SOUTH DAKOTA

WYOMING

IOWA

Get moving! I want to get to the end of the tour. That's when we get to munch on samples!

What's Made in Nebraska? Food products, chemicals, and machinery

Omaha •

Lincoln ★

Omaha has many telemarketing companies. These are companies that sell goods and services by phone.

MISSOURI

COLORADO

KANSAS

Weaver's Snacks makes cheese puffs, cheese snaps, corn chips, potato chips, and tortillas.

What's Mined in Nebraska? Petroleum and sand and gravel

Touring Weaver's Snacks in Lincoln

First you see crates of raw potatoes. You watch the potatoes get sliced and fried. Finally, you see bags filled with delicious potato chips. You're touring Weaver's Snacks in Lincoln!

Foods are Nebraska's major factory products. Food plants make cereal and animal food. Some make baked goods or dairy products.

Meatpacking is a huge Nebraska industry. Meatpacking plants cut and package beef and pork.

Chemicals are another important factory product. They include medicines, bug killers, and fertilizer. Many factories make farm machines, too.

Crunch, crunch! A worker makes potato chips at Weaver's Snacks.

The Hallmark Greeting Card Company began in Nebraska.

The Hand-Planted Forest near Halsey

Dr. Bessey sure had a green thumb! Be sure to visit Nebraska National Forest!

Dr. Charles Bessey taught at the University of Nebraska in Lincoln.

Have you ever planted a tree? It's not that easy to do. Just imagine planting a whole forest of trees! That's what Dr. Charles Bessey decided to do. He was a botanist, or plant scientist. He knew Nebraska's plains had few trees. He believed trees could grow in the sandy soil. So he decided to grow some.

Bessey's helpers planted thousands of trees. Those trees became the world's largest hand-planted forest. They were like a green island in the Sand Hills. They're now in Nebraska National Forest, near Halsey. Just climb up Scott Lookout Tower. You can look out over Bessey's dream!

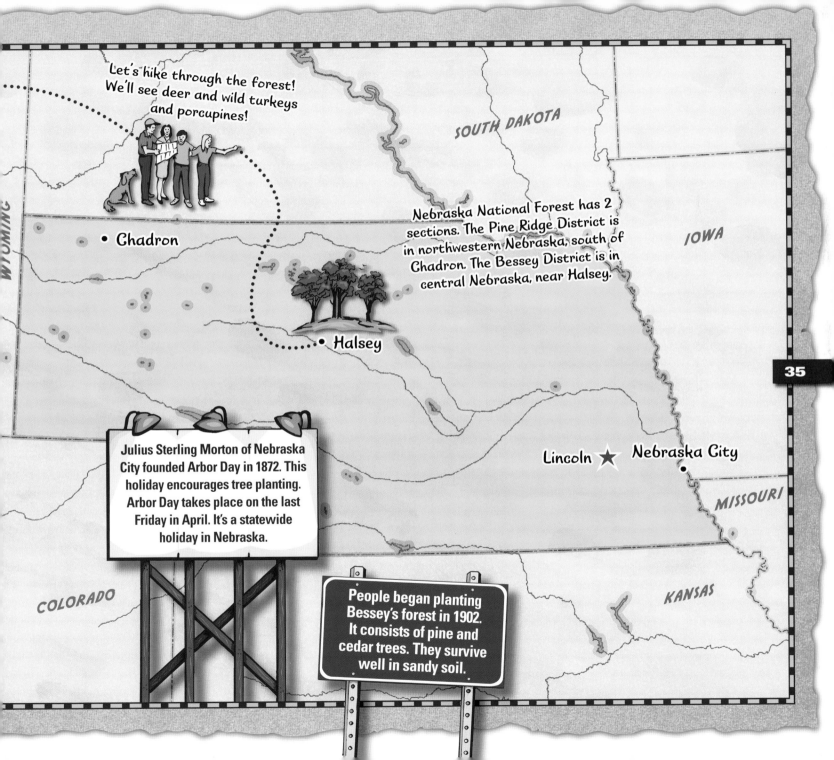

Let's hike through the forest! We'll see deer and wild turkeys and porcupines!

SOUTH DAKOTA

WYOMING

• Chadron

IOWA

Nebraska National Forest has 2 sections. The Pine Ridge District is in northwestern Nebraska, south of Chadron. The Bessey District is in central Nebraska, near Halsey.

• Halsey

Julius Sterling Morton of Nebraska City founded Arbor Day in 1872. This holiday encourages tree planting. Arbor Day takes place on the last Friday in April. It's a statewide holiday in Nebraska.

Lincoln ★ • Nebraska City

MISSOURI

COLORADO

People began planting Bessey's forest in 1902. It consists of pine and cedar trees. They survive well in sandy soil.

KANSAS

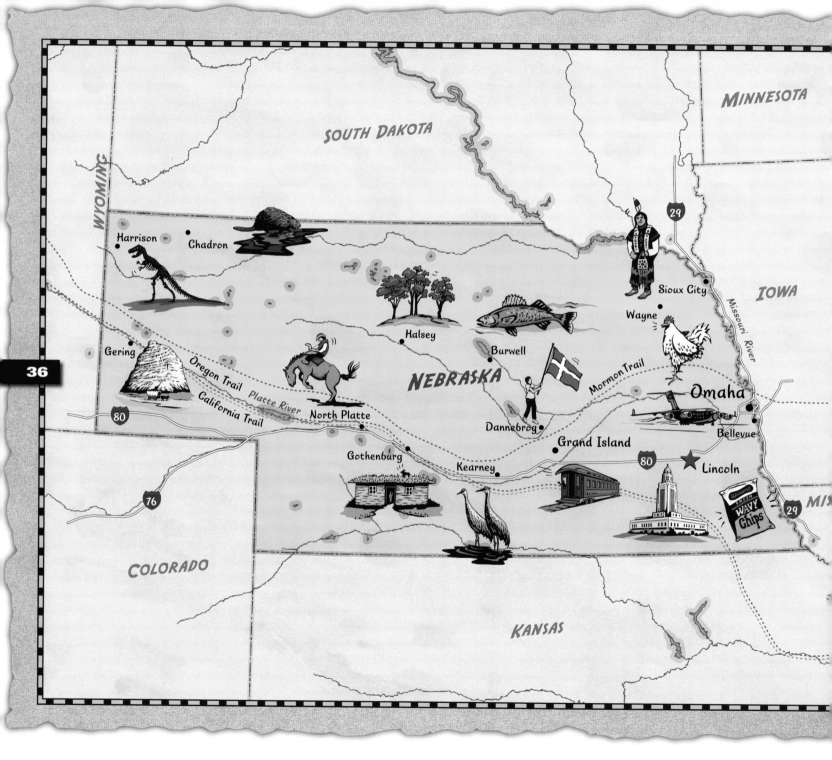

MINNESOTA

SOUTH DAKOTA

WYOMING

IOWA

Harrison   Chadron

Sioux City

Wayne

Gering

Halsey

Burwell

NEBRASKA

Missouri River

Omaha

Oregon Trail   Platte River

Mormon Trail

California Trail

North Platte

Dannebrog

Bellevue

Gothenburg

Kearney

Grand Island

Lincoln

WAVY Chips

COLORADO

KANSAS

MIS

80

76

80

29

29

OUR TRIP

We visited many amazing places on our trip! We also met a lot of interesting people along the way. Look at the map on the left. Use your finger to trace all the places we have been.

What did scientists find at Agate Fossil Beds? See page 6 for the answer.

How long do sandhill cranes live? Page 11 has the answer.

What is husking? See page 12 for the answer.

Who opened Fort Lisa? Look on page 19 for the answer.

Which trails did pioneers take through Nebraska? Page 21 has the answer.

What are Danish pancakes called? Turn to page 23 for the answer.

When was the transcontinental railroad completed? Look on page 24 and find out!

How many times did William Jennings Bryan run for president? Turn to page 30 for the answer.

That was a great trip! We have traveled all over Nebraska!

There are a few places that we didn't have time for, though. Next time, we plan to visit the Heartland of America Park in Omaha. This park is located along the Missouri River and features a lake, fountains, a waterfall, and walking path.

More Places to Visit in Nebraska

WORDS TO KNOW

broncos (BRONG-koz) wild or untrained horses

buckskins (BUHK-skinz) clothes made from the skin of a deer

drought (DROUT) a lack of rain

fossil (FOSS-uhl) a print or the remains of a plant or animal that lived long ago

headquarters (HED-kwor-turz) an organization's main office location

heritage (HER-uh-tij) customs passed down from earlier times

immigrants (IM-uh-gruhnts) people who leave their home country and settle in a new land

industries (IN-duh-streez) types of businesses

nuclear (NOO-klee-ur) producing energy from the splitting of tiny particles called atoms

pioneer (pye-uh-NEER) a person who moves into an unsettled land

skyscraper (SKYE-skray-pur) a very tall building

sod (SOD) chunks of earth with grass and roots attached

traditional (truh-DISH-uhn-ul) passed down from one generation to another

Nebraska covers 76,872 square miles (199,099 sq km). It's the 15th-largest state in size.

STATE SYMBOLS

State beverage: Milk

State bird: Western meadowlark

State fish: Channel catfish

State flower: Goldenrod

State folk dance: Square dance

State fossil: Mammoth

State gem: Blue chalcedony (blue agate)

State grass: Little bluestem

State insect: Honeybee

State mammal: White-tailed deer

State river: Platte River

State rock: Prairie agate

State soft drink: Kool-Aid

State soil: Holdrege series

State tree: Eastern cottonwood

State flag

State seal

STATE SONG

"Beautiful Nebraska"

Words by Jim Fras and Guy G. Miller, Music by Jim Fras

Beautiful Nebraska, peaceful prairieland,
Laced with many rivers, and the hills of sand;
Dark green valleys cradled in the earth,
Rain and sunshine bring abundant birth.
Beautiful Nebraska, as you look around,
You will find a rainbow reaching to the ground;
All these wonders by the Master's hand;
Beautiful Nebraska land.
We are so proud of this state where we live,
There is no place that has so much to give.

Beautiful Nebraska, as you look around,
You will find a rainbow reaching to the ground;
All these wonders by the Master's hand,
Beautiful Nebraska land.

FAMOUS PEOPLE

Abbott, Grace (1878–1939), social worker

Alexander, Grover Cleveland (1887–1950), baseball player

Astaire, Fred (1899–1987), dancer and actor

Baer, Max (1909–1959), boxer

Brando, Marlon (1924–2004), actor

Carson, Johnny (1925–2005), entertainer

Cheney, Richard (1941–), vice president to George W. Bush

Fonda, Henry (1905–1982), actor

Ford, Gerald (1913–), 38th U.S. president

Forrester, Jay W. (1918–), inventor

Hanson, Howard (1896–1981), composer

Kurtz, Swoozie (1944–), actor

La Flesche, Susette (1854–1903), American Indian rights activist and author

Leahy, Frank W. (1908–1973), football coach

Malcolm X (1925–1965), civil rights leader

Nolte, Nick (1940–), actor

Pound, Roscoe (1870–1964), educator

Red Cloud (1822–1909), American Indian chief

Standing Bear (ca. 1834–1908), American Indian chief

Wisniewski, David (1953–2002), children's author, illustrator

Zanuck, Darryl F. (1902–1979), film producer

TO FIND OUT MORE

At the Library

Fradin, Dennis Brindell. *Nebraska*. Chicago: Children's Press, 1995.

McLeese, Don. *Red Cloud*. Vero Beach, Fla.: Rourke Publishing, 2004.

Sandburg, Carl, and David Small (illustrator). *The Huckabuck Family and How They Raised Popcorn in Nebraska and Quit and Came Back*. New York: Farrar Strauss Giroux, 1999.

Shepherd, Rajean Luebs, and Sandy Appleoff (illustrator). *C Is for Cornhusker: A Nebraska Alphabet*. Chelsea, Mich.: Sleeping Bear Press, 2004.

On the Web

Visit our home page for lots of links about Nebraska:
http://www.childsworld.com/links

Note to Parents, Teachers, and Librarians: We routinely verify our Web links to make sure they are safe, active sites—so encourage your readers to check them out!

Places to Visit or Contact

Nebraska Department of Economic Development, Tourism Division
PO Box 98907
Lincoln, NE 68509-8907
877/632-7275
For more information about traveling in Nebraska

Nebraska State Historical Society
PO Box 82554
Lincoln, NE 68501-2554
402/471-3270
For more information about the history of Nebraska

INDEX

Bye, Cornhusker State.
We had a great time.
We'll come back soon!

40